T0090789

LOVE POEMS

AND OTHER THINGS

David D Plain

Order this book online at www.trafford.com
or email orders@trafford.com

Most Trafford titles are also available at major online book retailers.

Print information available on the last page.

ISBN: 978-1-6987-1162-1 (sc)
ISBN: 978-1-6987-1161-4 (e)

Trafford rev. 03/30/2022

www.trafford.com
North America & international
toll-free: 844-688-6899 (USA & Canada)
fax: 812 355 4082

This work is dedicated to my writer compatriots who have helped me grow throughout my writing endeavours.

Contents

A Guest Poem

I met John B Lee for the first time at a book launch in Sarnia, Ontario. A mutual friend introduced us. We subsequentially discovered that John had a keen interest in indigenous history. After sharing some history of the area, he sent me this poem he had written in our meeting's honour. John is Poet Laureate of the city of Brantford in perpetuity, Poet Laureate of Norfolk County for Life, Poet Laureate of the Canada Cuba Literary Alliance (CLAA) 2020-2022.

He Tells Me[1]

he tells me
of an ancient burial mound
on the banks of the Thames
near present day Pain Court - his Ojibwa ancestors
lacing their bones in the earth
reaching through life
like the most common roots of lives once lived

he tells me
in the war
of the confederacy
of the three fires
how his people
tore the arms and legs
away from the corpses
of the vanquished Iroquois
how they decapitated these Seneca foe
burning their longhouses scouring their village
how they scattered

---

[1]   Printed with permission.

disfigured bodies
like a whirlwind come to a fractured forest

so that in the afterlife
they might not
gather back the spirits
of the fallen and unenduring enemy

their souls tattered
like rain-torn smoke
thinned to nothing by bad weather
and the hissing away of wet burn
he tells me
his grandfather's great grandfather
was once a war chief
in that old
victory over time
that comes to the knowing

and last evening
in the late afternoon before our talk
I walked
my local streets in Port Dover
down Richardson past Aaron
left onto Denby
to Mergyl then home
along Nelson
and it was such a lovely
leaf-whipped autumn
perhaps the last

of the good days
before winter
lost faith with the sun
and I saw
one leaf rise
out of the bustling multitude
catching itself
like something solitary
something joyful
in the multifarious hordes
of vanquished beauty
and comes home memory
comes home dream
and I would think of this
unblooming
this shattering sky
even as this good man
tells me
his own heroic story
of the doomed ghosts of a glorious war

and I hope
I am also that
one lonesome leaf
lifting its voice
through blue silence
and drifting off into darkness
yet to come
miles from the fire
catching my feet

in the crimson rumour of this dying hour
when the spirit
of every broken thing
finds an everlasting champion
gone ahead, left behind
and quietly waiting

John B. Lee

A Lament for Impractical Passion

This poem is a lament written for an older man and his feelings of love for a young woman.

One lonely dewdrop
kisses thirsty petal
sweet liquid plies fragrant rose.
They live together,
at this moment.
Live in the present.
Each the same age.
With that kiss, they become one.

But not for us,
this union of two lovers.
I am from long ago.
Now aged. Now spent.
And you, my love,
the object of my futile hope.
You are from the future.

Yet our timeless souls still touch,
presently binding us together.

You possess youth's fleeting beauty,
while mine has faded in distant days.
Your shining star beams brilliant,
its radiance a blinding light.
Mine weakened to a wispy glow.

We come from different eras,
preventing hands from reaching out,
lips from pressing new wine,
while amorous nectar drips syrupy honey.
Your atlas of life lay stretched before you,
while I look back at roads well travelled.

Unlike that drop and petal,
whose kiss initiates their souls' entanglement.
Preparing to vanquish incessant difficulties.
Consuming issues of the day.

My body grows old, and time separates
with a distance that can't be bridged.
But the heart stays ever young.
Oh, sorrowful pain for things
that will never be!

A Tale of Two Women

The two women in this poem are my grandmother and her experiences with World War I and my mother and her experiences with World War II.

The archduke is dead. The war has begun.
Two lovers are split until it is done.
Four years in the mud while she waits alone.
Love mingles now we no longer postpone

Lovely daughters in two moments appear,
two years apart…now the reaper is near.
What in God's green earth am I doing here
Tubes up my nose, and a beep in my ear?

Wires all over me, analyzing my chest.
Two ears are listening to hear my request.
Blurred vision tells me it's her sitting there
across from my bed in one lonely chair.

My fate is consumption; my spirit's not blithe.
I have little choice, a date with his scythe.
A few breaths but left and me in my prime.
This wretched disease... I want some more time!

My voice is raspy my throat; I can't clear.
Come close, I whisper; I need you near here.
I've something to say before I depart.
It's something I've thought of close to my heart.

My life's been wonderful sharing with you.
Can you forgive me and still love me too?
I've failed you, my love, much to my dismay.
I'm sorry I'm sick; I hate being this way.

Painful ears listen with a raw, broken heart
to comforting words... Why are we apart?
Time starts its healing, near two decades pass.
Peace feigned in speeches as his troops amass!

Her daughter enlists, the world's come undone.
Now Panzer divisions... blitzkrieg's begun.
This lightning war seems to come at no cost.
He rolls over France, and Europe is lost.

England still stands but falls under the blitz.
As underground clubs perform big band hits
for those who are weary and live out each day,
meeting their lovers, the flyboys who stay

For only a short time…they're off again
into the blackness till darkness should wane.
Then dawn's first twilight sees most safe return;
straight to the club, where she waits with concern.

She spots him arrive her heart skips a beat;
dashingly handsome, his stature's complete.
They embrace, then they dance. The hours are few.
They share precious time; love's tenderness is due.

Alas, one dark morn while she waited there,
alone her thoughts vex, there's his vacant chair.
It sits forlornly where it will remain.
He failed to arrive…would never again.

Always

Always is a poem written about a wedding day and a hint of things to come. The groom's brother sang the song *Always* at the reception accompanied by his ukulele.

Surveyed through eyes
not blurred by time,
an age long past,
a canvas splashed
with vivid colour.

When vows declared
and church bells tolled—the news.

Benedictions pronounced,
Toasts delivered.
And a ukulele accompanied…
Always.

That nocturnal hour appeared.
The espoused stole off

to consummate the nuptials,
and play among the stars.

Drifting off to paradise,
cheating, so it seemed,
a certain Hooded Skeleton,
the one that holds the keys.

Life's banquet table now
lay stretched before
the youthful dyad,
a smorgasbord of hopeful dreams
and sanguine plans.

A lifetime stole by
with stealthy diversions.
Stealing opportunities to actualize
those confident intentions.

Now a caveat!
A message to the past.
Be wary not to cast
your infant deep-felt love
upon Moloch's sacrificial fire.

Angel on a Train

Angel on a Train tells the story of a love encounter on a VIA train bound for Toronto.

Boarded the big blue and yellow.
Tapping in time to a subtle bolero.
Took my seat just before six,
hypnotic trance by rhythmic clicks.

Each clack a painful reminder,
of broken faith, a trust placed in error.
Of a broken heart that pains my soul,
a shipwreck stuck on life's gravel shoal.

Inner eyes were glazed.
My soul is crazed.
My soul is dazed.
My soul is dazed.

While I languished, my spirit prone,
my heart, it fluttered, the sun, it shone.

There you sat beautifully stunning,
your perfume light not overpowering.

I gasped for breath; depression fled.
Your beauty daunts regard of dread,
to go where genial health will profit.
Desire released my shipwrecked spirit.

Inner eyes were glazed.
My soul is dazed.
My soul is amazed.
My soul is amazed.

I stared at you. You glanced at me.
I turned away. I could not see.
I peeked at you, you turned away.
Time to move, cannot delay.

Alluring eyes lock, tempting fate,
to join in a rapturous debate.
The whole trip spent in spoken word,
no click, no clack was ever heard

Inner eyes were glazed.
My soul is dazed.
My soul is amazed.
My soul is amazed.
Jaunt now ended, we disembark.
Exchange phone numbers with no remark.

A long embrace, a tender kiss,
your company I'll sorely miss.

Into the night you disappear,
without a word, but it is clear.
Love's magic happened betwixt the twain,
because of the Angel on a Train.

Another Sabbath

Another Sabbath is a poem about the aftermath of a broken marriage, psychological pain and self-medication with alcohol and random sexual encounters.

Another Sabbath.
Sun has set,
five days' labour—*fini*.
"The eagle has shit."

Boys' night out.
Young men prowl.
Bending elbows,
chasing poon.

Girls' night out.
Young women stray.
Flashing smiles
that flaunt availability.

Showered and shaved.
Fragrant cologne.
Manly sweet hook
to temp the booty.

Blind Pig beckons.
Colonial bids.
Round follows round.
Pub after pub.
Paycheque melts.
Night drags on.

Dust-up breaks out.
Spills out *Morden's*
dark exit.
Blowhard caves.
I move on.
Colony Bar calls.
Ex and new beau,
across hazy room.
Heart breaking.
They bolt.

In fog-laden memory
Red Shingle appears.
Shoot a little stick,
make a little coin.

Night is spent.
House lights flash

last call.
Hope fades.
Elusive hookup eludes.

End of the line.
White Mary's:
pit's bottom.

Gorgeous blonde?
Attractive brunette?
Redheaded beauty?
Soothing balm.

I place a twenty
in White Mary's hand.

Arkona Shale

Arkon Shale is a poem about one of Canada's best geological spots to collect fossils; Arkona, Bosanquet Township, Lambton County, Ontario.

Nestled beside Bosanquet
crossing Sylvan Road
a deep ravine runs.

By creator's vision
relentless Ausable River
forms beauty.

Rushing waters
over boulders strewn.
Rapids lay bare
Devonian remnants.

Fossil Road leads
to current so swift.

Stony shore reveals
the formation's pure treasuries.

Thin black shale
between layered limestone
presents fossiliferous trove.

Stooping collectors
know this hidden place—Hungry Hollow.

Clerihew Poems

The Clerihew Poem:

- It is a whimsical, four-line *biographical poem* invented by Edmund Clerihew Bentley in 1905.
- The first line is the name of the poem's subject. Usually, a famous person is put in an absurd light (and humourous).
- The rhyme scheme is AABB, and the rhymes are often forced.
- The line length and metre are irregular.

The clerihew poem has also, occasionally, been used for non-biographical verses too.

I went to the powwow

Although I don't know how now

To drum or dance

So, I should have gone to France!

They looked for the man in the hat

Who's just a rat

Who bombed the airport in Brussels
That takes no muscles.

This man called Abraham Lincoln
His team was stinkin
Negotiating a backroom deal
The presidency to steal!

Cool Desperado: The Ballad of Eddie Boyd

Robing the poor while riding the rails
Averting restraint in cold steel jails
A gas station stick-up his haul was naught
Save a stretch in the clink; Eddie's been caught!

Felon in training at the grey bar hotel
Saskatchewan's best; it replicates hell
Thirty short months, then out on parole
War's broken out should Eddie enrol?

A long tour in Europe, the war has been won
Shipped home and discharged, the commando is done
He tries to go straight, but life is too boring
Now a gangsters' life, the thrill would be roaring!

Groomed for the fast lane
A gun in his hand!
Yes, groomed for the fast lane
A gun in his hand!

His father a cop and religious too!
But not for Eddie, to himself, he'll be true
Edwin Alonzo Boyd; a cool desperado
He'll rob a bank, flee in his auto!

Groomed for the fast lane
A gun in his hand!
Yes, groomed for the fast lane
A gun in his hand!

He avoided the law at least for a time
Caught then locked up for his bank-robbing crime
There in the dank Don Jail, he met
The Jackson boys, but a quartet not yet.

A hacksaw blade most cleverly hidden
In Lennie's prosthetic, their escape is now bidden
Over the wall and up the Don Valley
Their flight now complete, and four would now rally!

Scoundrels and scalawags
Folk heroes become.
Yes, scoundrels and scalawags
Folk heroes become.

Petty Thief Suchan now joined the three
The Boyd Gang would go on a bank-robbing spree
Adored by the public, loved by the press
Back to the slammer for crimes they confess.

A second hacksaw smuggled in by a lawyer
Helped set them free, but the bunch would fracture
Eddie laid low in a flat in Toronto
Captured again cause the cops knew what condo

Scoundrels and scalawags
Folk heroes become.
Yes, scoundrels and scalawags
Folk heroes become.

The Jackson named Willie fled to old Montreal
Hiding out on the lam where he'd meet his downfall
While the other two bolt to a Montreal suburb
After killing a cop at a Toronto street curb.

The romance had ended
The pleasure suspended
The public's offended
A hanging's demanded.

To prison with all
And hang the cop killers!
Yes, prison for all
And hang the cop killers!

Suchan and Lennie, the murdering duo
Arrested, sent back for a stint on death row
Convicted, appointed a time at Don's gallows
Lennie would hop to the neck-stretching maestro

To prison with all
And hang the cop killers!
Yes, prison for all
And hang the cop killers!

Our hero Eddie and his old friend Willie
Are back in Don Jail, where cells are so chilly
Sentenced long stretches in Kingston's big house
When Eddie's paroled, he's mild as a mouse.

But the Gang's charming leader
Has still got pizzazz!
Yes, the Gang's charming leader
Has still got pizzazz!

After a long spell in that infamous pen
Eddie's released, paroled yet again
He moved to the west coast, he quietly retired
To live out his life with stories that transpired.

But the Gang's charming leader
Has still got pizzazz!
Yes, the Gang's charming leader
Has still got pizzazz!

Dance of the Pulsars

This sonnet describes an astrological event known as a nova, an explosion that occurs in a white-dwarf star in a binary system.

Expansive void oh so voluminous,
is where I live and work oblivious,
to a wandering star, my orb draws in,
to circle, to dance, to become my twin.

Oh, deadly dance. Your deathly spiral
lurking behind love's crafty recital.
Imitating pleasure, a toxic embrace.
Dual suns duelling, inhibitions unlace.

Emotions emit like mass ejections,
mingling along with sensual unctions.
The two at rest in placid enjoyment,
each never knowing a rose so fragrant.

That void, now filled with stellar aurora,
abruptly over. A tragic nova.

Departure Imminent

**Departure Imminent is a poem explaining the
author's understanding of the meaning of death.**

Within this husk
dwells a timeless essence.
Trapped within Einstein's monstrosity,
bonded to his time/space milieu,
pulled toward an untimely end.

Trapped with eyes
that do not close.
Forced to watch intimate familiars
thrash against the force
of time's relentless current,
pushing this form through
space's infinitude.

Time is no friend,
stealing your youth.
Leaving behind

a lump of aching
muscle and bone.
Life's verve spent
by the tide of time.
It can only flow.
It cannot ebb.

Look upstream!
At those who are
behind your journey.
Youth, busily trying
to build a lasting monument
that cannot last.
Impervious how far along
the torrent has carried them.

Departure imminent.
Releasing these bonds,
not by one's hand but
Providence will choose.
Time will end.
Space will be no more.

A daunting vault.
A lonely leap.
Multitudes have taken,
many will follow.
There is no choice.
Time's end will come.
It pushed you to this place.

Return to the twelfth dimension.
A place that has no space,
no time to hinder.
No somatic confinement
to deteriorate,
a place where all belong—Hallelujah!

Destination Instant

Destination Instant depicts the leap from last breath to next life, the time it takes and its location.

Eyes now closed,
drifting into a coma,
motionlessly consuming.
Darkness abides.

Departure point is here,
also destination.
Time is instant
and space exists no more.

Corporeal nescience closed off,
incorporeal awareness turned on.
Essence now simmering energy,
a quivering closed hoop.

Cognizance begins.
Duality stops.

Static residence
at quantum's nether regions.

Blinding light
bathes with knowledge.
Consciousness adjusts
by the sentient inner eye.

Now subordinate
to atom's basal members.
Whizzing point particles
prodigiously apparent.

Tinier even still
as though to fill
the cosmos
and stimulate satiation.

Light and soul become one,
pure energy.
Oscillations endure.
Now volume surpasses all.

Sentience everlasting.
Macrocosm's fabric,
vibrating strings singing
Creator's praises.

Choirs vocalize
ethereal hymns.

Resounding songs
which have no words.

Overwhelming joy
inundates void
where adversity cannot enter.
Destination instant!

Diamante Poems

A diamante poem is a poem that makes the shape of a diamond. The poem compares two different subjects. They are named in one word in the first and last lines. The second line consists of two adjectives describing the subject. The third line contains three verbs ending in the suffix "ing," related to the subject. A fourth line then has four nouns related to the subject, but only the first two words are associated with the first subject. The other two words describe the opposite subject. The lines are reversed, leading to either a second subject or a synonym for the first.

The poem may also compare the two subjects named in the first and last lines. There are two synonyms in the second line and three in the third line. The first two words in the fourth line are synonyms for the first subject, and the last two words are antonyms. Line five has three antonyms, line six has two.

Youth
Energy Stamina
Running Skating Clubbing
Athletic Beauty Resigned Retired

Fatiguing Receding Sleeping
Worn Done
Senior

Faith
Trust Belief
Hope Loyalty Truth
Assent Conviction Doubt Disbelief
Denial Uncertainty Rejection
Skepticism Misgiving
Mistrust

End to a Romance

Tender June evening,
when we shared a moment.
A dinner for two
on a warm summer evening.

Fall colours herald
An end to the summer
An end to a romance
An end to a friendship.

Longing eyes looking
And wanting lips pressing
While fingertips touching
Cascading together.

Fall colours herald
An end to the summer
An end to a romance
An end to a friendship.

Ice cream and French fries
A rain-soaked free concert
And long walks at sunset
And searches for beaches.

Fall colours herald
An end to the summer
An end to a romance
An end to a friendship.

A weekend in heaven
A search for perfection
A fleeting three days
Still reaches an apex.

Fall colours herald
An end to the summer
A romance that's ended
An end to a friendship.

Entanglement Denied

This sonnet portrays a close encounter with an illicit affair that doesn't come to fruition due to high morals.

Time to move on. Who's this? She's an angel.
Sent from nirvana, her allure is contagious.
A radiant smile with sparkling eyes,
and smooth silken skin, my emptiness dies.
With an angelic voice, she lifts my esteem.
Her loving concern exhorts me to dream.

Polite exchange to friendly devotion.
Celestial charm gives rise to passion.
The long conversation leading to interest
in clandestine love, my adverse dearest.
But crossing thin line, a slip and a fall,
annulling ardour and life's curtain call.

Noble rectitude denies wanton lure.
Averting the life of a loathed paramour.

First Contact

First Contact is a poem about the arrival of Europeans upon the shores of North America and the advice given by a sage, spiritual guide.

Brilliant globe
displays his face.
Calefacient crown
peeking o'er sea's plane
breaking horizon.
Ambience illuminated
by rising grandfather
leaving behind the briny deep.

Ritual performed
without exception,
every morn without decline,
creating each day anew.
Except for this day
he drags behind

a vision rising
from watery expanse.

White clouds billow
to carry out
a singular duty.
This wooden vessel's
ever-increasing volume.
Till anchor drops and
small boats kiss
mother's rugged shore.

Now strange men stand
upon the rocky crop.
Foretold from eons past.
Lustrous messengers from the sea,
speaking through sacred megis shell,
a prophecy of expectation,
of strangers' sojourn
from sea to land.

Accept the curious,
lambent one implores.
Faces hairy whose hue
apes the look
of grandmother moon.
Gnosis of the soul is
cradled by Spirit.
Utilize your inviting nature.

Flocking Blackbirds

Blackbirds: a gathering.
Several hundred or a thousand
congregate in tall, mature poplars…
an avian invisibleness in the evening twilight.
Except the branches dance with incessant squawking.
A noise most deafening.

Without warning: abandonment.
They leave each steady perch,
group after group, taking flight.
The dusky sky turns a darker shade
as the airborne flock grows.
And circles my deck
a din of ominous things to come.

Of falling leaves and dull, grey skies,
and air that shows the breath,
itself a prophecy of descent
into the harshness of winter.
That season of white with the need for gloves,

and scarves and bulky, thick suits.
Bundled bodies, protection from icy atmosphere.

But also, a season of roaring fires,
of holly, pine cones and coloured lights.
Sounds of festive conversation
float through the home.
Delicious aromas intermingle in the air,
freshly popped corn, fudge bubbling on the range.
The romantic mistletoe that calls young lovers
to hold each other close, a tender kiss,
then leave the warmth of the hearth
for a moonlit ride, the jingling of a one-horse sleigh
announcing a new found love.

Florido

Bleak winds blow cold
across barren landscape
north of the 49th.
Snowbirds look longingly south.

Mangrove forests are filled with trees.
Eyes look skyward with great expectation.
Invasion begins. Blue turns white.
Sails billow. Descendants land.

Sail down black bitumen river
courtesy of poisonous tar sands.
Thickened and laid long
the length of the tripper's peninsula.

Travel a narrow corridor
rimmed by the fragrant orchid.
Through rising steam once deluge
released by thunderous claps.

Green groves burst with spots of orange.
Fields of fruit ripened red on the vine.
Fields that stretch to reach the glades,
a harvest to feed a nation.

Residents most temporary
plant happy feet
upon *Florido's* soil
to taste key lime pie and lemonade.

Antagonist winter turns summer lover
to white shell beaches on the gulf.
Gold coast beckons, and tourists flock
as musicians play well into the night.

Goddess of Liberty

There she stands, the Goddess from France,
proclaiming liberty, a scowl on her face.
Surveying domain with blank glare staring,
dead eyes that gaze at desolation she'll wreak.

More illegals, to add to the millions,
stand by her side stare at her face.
Illegal settlers and squatters who steal,
mountains and rivers and valleys, not theirs.

Build a wall! Build it higher!
There are rapists among them!
They rape their own mother!
Scarring her beauty, shaving her head!

Polluting her body with ribbons of asphalt.
Oil streams flow through lines of cold steel
that crisscross her torso, once clothed in foliage
producing clean air—no longer can breathe.

Once loving parent nurturing her children,
children whose warriors can no longer shield
life-giving earth from their toxic arrows;
destructive missiles that poison clear water.

Oh, Statue of Liberty, live we beseech you!
Seventh Fire is done; the Eighth has been lit.
Give us liberty and life; your children choose,
unholy invaders, the decision is yours.

Turn from illusion, from material things.
Embrace our ancestors' spiritual way.
We all shall live; our mother will heal.
The path we are on leads only to death.

Hope Abounds

Failure is our lot!
Life
has produced no wisdom,
nor any sensibility.
That wall that separates
gives opportunity and
the headbangers
try, try, try again,
to no avail.

Achievement gives way
and all is lost.
Try again.
To love,
to succeed.
But no, we are out of balance.
Spiritual beings
ignoring immortality while
pursuing mortality.

We are wanderers
unable to find our way.
We embrace devolution
and call it enlightenment.
Grasp knowledge and
denigrate faith.
Secular thought has no future.
Technology smothers,
leading to perdition.

But hope abounds,
for we are kept
in the deep niche
of the mind of God.
And hidden
in the recesses
of our souls
resides longing
for the one that is.

Just a Few Limericks

I wrote these limericks in 2016 in response to a contest offered by 'Cadence: a reading series with some music, Sarnia, ON Canada'

An old man once entered a contest
To write a limerick, most honest
But the thing was so bad
It made everyone sad
So he left town now he's the gonest!

An old man once viewed a young beauty
Whose voluptuous boobs were just hooty
He thought with a drool
That life was so cruel
As she walked past, he just watched her booty.

There once was a man named The Donald
Who stared and young women were ogled
Who ran for an office
But he had no compass
He looked more like Ronald McDonald.

There once was a woman named Hillary
Whose opponents would often call Killary
She went off the rez
And ran to be Prez
After speaking, they all called her Shrillary

There once was a poet named John
Whose ditties went on and on
But they do tell a story
With none of them hoary
And I know they'll be published by dawn.

I once knew a girl who read
A novel that turned her face red
She read it straight through
Her libido just flew
Vibrator on high it sure sped!

More Limericks

These limericks are based on the adage "You Can Lead a Horse to Water, But You Can't Make Him Drink."

There once was a man from Toronto
Whose habits were disliked and pronto
He bent his elbow too oft
His language became too unsoft
So, we drowned him in the Gulf of Lepanto.

A man once had such a habit
It made him act like a rabbit
Stop we implored
Too oft you have scored
So, we sent him off to the abbot.

They say that pot is a gateway
To a life that will end with may-day
Your teeth and hair will fall out
Your sanity, you surely will doubt
But deliverance is found with the padre.

Nonsensical

An anagram poem:

1. Choose a single-word title (long words are better; eleven or more letters).
2. Find as many words as you can within that title that contain four letters or more (smaller words aren't allowed because it makes it far too easy).
3. Write a poem with the same number of lines as letters in the title. Each line must end
4. with one of the words you found (contained within your title word), and the poem should address the subject content in the title. No two lines may end with the same word. You cannot add any suffix, prefix, or other ending (*i.e., -s* or *-ing* or *-ed*

At last, we are alone
No obstacle in our lane
No need to cross the line
Temptation? There is none.

Once stripped, candy cane
Sweeter than chocolate cone
Keep in line with the law of canon
Fire roars from the mouth of the cannon!

We loved but once
When we sailed the Blue Nile
Our love to mast we did nail!

Ode to Vimy

I wrote this ode to commemorate the Battle of Vimy Ridge, April 9-12, 1917.

In dank, cold caverns
upon Spartan walls,
names and dates etched
by warriors each,
while waiting, the canons
of arms and charge,
to take the hill,
one-forty-five.

French ridge eternal
surveys Douai,
a gentle plain that lay before
the zealous Hun
who exploits his mines
and runs his factories full.

Relentless barrage
battered the rim.
Defences disabled
on predominate reports
from bi-winged recon.

The boys from the colony
forged by Somme's ordeal,
now rehearse, rehearse,
yet again, rehearse.
While twelve deep subways
sappers built, a sheltered
network, a cold respite.

Prepare for that edict
old men would order.
To battle young men!
Move out to the saps
sealed off at their ends.
Leave behind
Zivy's cool shelter.

Grandfathers and greats
arise to the call
that came at last.
Rise and charge
and taunt the Reaper's face.

A gentle slope,
it is no friend.

It benefits the foe.
Who stares down its long incline
through sights aimed
between the barbs.

Easter Monday—'tis sunless.
Warm *helios* awaits
biting storm borne
on April's gale.

Saps' caps blew
and gallant colonials
spilled out.
Into Europe's perdition,
that mud-soaked landscape
pocked by cannons' craters.

Stinging sleet amidst the snow
carried by a nor'west howl
swept their purview
that raw spring morn.
A friend indeed.

Pimple's projectiles spray
the braveheart
and the gallant.
Innocent boys who came
so far from home
to taste victory's
sweet nectar.

Now comrades fall while
those who stand inch forward
one hundred paces to the blast.

Repeat, repeat until the noon
when most has been accomplished,
One-forty-five remains another day,
its defence is resolute.
Until at last, the mount is wholly theirs.

Success has earned
its line upon
Versailles' accord.
Vimy Ridge has birthed
a nation new.
Canada now takes its place—
Colonials no more!

One Last Wish

This sonnet is dedicated to my grandparents, who were young lovers when World War I broke out. He shipped out. She waited faithfully for his return. When he did, they married and had two daughters. When they were ages four and two, he became ill with tuberculosis and died in a sanitarium. It was written before *A Tale of Two Women*, to which I added her oldest daughter's story.

What in God's green earth am I doing here?
Tubes up my nose, and a beep in my ear,
Wires all over-analyzing my chest
Two ears are listening to hear my request.

Blurred vision tells me it's her sitting there
Across from my bed in one lonely chair
My voice is raspy my throat I can't clear
Come close, I whisper, I need you near here

I've something to say before I depart
It's something I've thought of close to my heart

My life's been a wonder sharing with you.
Can you forgive me and still love me too?
I've failed you, my love, much to my dismay
I'm sorry I'm sick, hate being this way.

Phases of Being

This sonnet describes the different stages of life from youth to middle-age through senior citizenship.

Youthful passion fills the springtime of life.
The future belongs; there be zero strife.
Then melts like spring snow under April sun,
where now 'tis tempered, maturing begun.

This rising sun now approaches zenith
displays its splendour a bright behemoth.
Now begins to fade, yet star still dazzles.
Spent time used well; time left are equal.

Now future abridged, sunsets in the west,
busily using the time that is left.
Marking this present moment by moment,
now rushing of time a fear doth foment,
lasts but a short spell, tranquil days now spend.
Pattern now holding, awaiting the end.

Reconciliation Realized

Reconciliation with Canada's Indigenous peoples is something the people of the wider society are exploring. This poem presents a possible solution, a way to achieve it finally.

Aanii! *Boozhoo*!
A welcoming salutation
to strangers whose long sojourn
by *jiimaan*[2], driven by billowing clouds,
has brought them to our shores.

Come, rest upon our mats,
shelter yourselves in our lodges,
renew your strength with food,
quench your thirst with clear, pure water.
Creator's gifts are yours as well.

No!
Not ours as well,
but all is ours.

---

[2]   Jiimaan = Ojibwa for canoe

Now to justify
our appropriation.

Terra Nullius—an option!
From that old Roman edict—
Dwellers, unlike us,
not human beings.
The land is empty.

More is required.
Moral justification,
to cover our sins.
Look to the Church.
A papal bull, maybe two!

Yes, Bulls of Discovery
Romanus Pontifex
conquer, colonize and exploit
non-Christian nations
and their lands.

Inter Caetera
Subjugate discovered peoples.
Bring them to the faith!
Propagate the Christian Empire.
Radical title is born!

O Crown, turn from your arrogant ways!
Courts of learned men, reject your biased views!
Is it greed perhaps,

or love of power
that blinds you?

Your highest court decreed:
It is understood that the Crown
acquired underlying title
when it asserted sovereignty
over lands, not theirs.

Understood? By whom?
By the ones with the power
to take by force.
Coercion is your character.
Is reconciliation beyond reach?

It only comes through equality.
Reject *Terra Nullius*.
Cast-off Doctrines of Discovery.
Live up to our treaties, share Radical Title,
Reconciliation realized!

Reversing Falls

This free verse poem explains the cause of the Reversing Falls on the St. John River, New Brunswick, Canada, from its beginning in the South Indian Ocean.

Grandmother moon works her powerful forces
on an orchestra of ocean tides
conducted by her compelling pull.
First, she tugs at South Indian waters
drawing higher each mile she moves.

Rotating west, she rounds the cape
across mother earth's second surface.
Stacked upon Atlantic seas.
She sends Fundy Bay awash,
awash in briny water.

Rushing headlong up the bay
three stories high and moving fast
to clash with one so mighty.

Saline mixes with fresh, natural confluent.
The mighty St. John begins to yield.

Duelling currents contend directions.
One flows up, the other down.
At first, a winner there seems not,
an hour's third, and all is calm.
Then upward bound the deluge sweeps.

Up the gorge, it flows near three leagues,
reversing now timid river's flow.
High tide brings forth nature's wonder,
spectacular vista, striking scene,
water-level panorama!

Sensual Summer

Sensual Summer is a sonnet reminiscing a summer love affair.

Warm June evening, you shared my reading.
A dinner for two, hot summer evening,
sensual petting, climax, then stroking
each other's soft skin, atmosphere soaking.

Summer festivals enjoyed together,
First Fridays, powwows, the summer weather.
Ice cream and French fries, a rain-soaked concert
with interludes of intimate lovemaking covert.

Sunsets along river's parkway at dusk,
smoothies at Timmy's their pastries a must.
Searching out Huron's finest sand beaches.
Ardent get-a-way, apex now reaches.

Leaving fall colours heralding an end
to sensual summer, with tears to spend.

Stuck in the Snow

This poem is the result of an exercise to write a poem or short story based on a selection of answers to the following questions: Name a number from one to ten, a personal name starting with the letter S, a colour, a musical instrument and one of your physical attributes.

For **seven** long winters, I've toiled to grow,
searching for signs for the end of the snow.
The time of my life I desire is spring,
to be like my big sister, that's this girl's thing.

My dumb parents named me a name oh so dumb!
Sharon, they called me old-fashioned to some.
Why not Traci but Sharon? I hate it so.
Sharon, it might as well have been Joe!

My thoughts return to my sister and beau,
who played in a rock band at Friday night's show.
He was so cool playing songs oh so **blue**.
I'm overlooked, my big sister he'd woo.

He'd practice at my house, he and his band.
In the garage, the sound was so grand.
When his **sax** would wail, my young heart would melt
My crush on this teen boy was truly heartfelt

The lead singer was big sis, plus guitar and drum
When they played together, would make me sure hum
My sister was Sue, and his name was Gary
The only thing better was ice cream and berry!

I struggle with that; what's my greater wish?
Enamoured with Gary or ice cream in a dish.
I didn't dwell long or ponder this quandary
I'm still **short** on years, besides there is Andre!

Summer Paramour

Summer Paramour is a sonnet longingly recalling a long-ago illicit affair that lasted only a summer.

Tender June evening, a dinner for two.
Fingertips touching, caressing debut.
A rain-soaked concert searches for beaches.
Long walks at sunset, a feeling that reaches
apex of love, a sun-splashed vacation,
brief bliss but then a hint of cessation.

Once I belonged, and once you were mine.
Lonely souls mingle 'till the end of time.
Amour forever, but no, it's over.
All are now thorns, once covered in clover.
Melancholy heart, melancholy pain,
sunshine is fleeting; it gives way to rain.

Fall colours herald an end to summer,
and romance, friendship, the loss of a lover.

Sure Am Missin You Today

This poem is my attempt at songwriting.

Sure am missin you today
I'm so sad you went away
I don't think you're comin back
Sure am missin you today

    Melancholy heart
    Melancholy anguish
    Hopeless misery
    Sleepless nights are here to stay

Loved your body next to mine
I loved you all the time
Loved your kisses, wrappin tongues
Sure am missin you today

    Melancholy heart
    Melancholy anguish

Hopeless misery
Just driving me insane

I was yours, and you were mine
Were together all the time
You made me feel so complete
Sure am missin you today

Melancholy heart
Melancholy anguish
Hopeless misery
Leading only to despair

How it hurts to realize
Our love was only lies
Once I pleased you but no more
Sure am missin you today

Melancholy heart
Melancholy torment
Hopeless misery
Life's become an empty place

You no longer care for me
You've moved on it's plain to see
Nothin left for me to do
Sure am missin you today

Tahitian Dream

The auburn-haired lady I wrote this for is now a white-haired lady.

Mist shrouded vessel,
dawn's early morn.
The fog soon lifts,
The mainsail's torn.

Sounding from the bow
on the three-masted vessel.
An island appears
for the good ship to nestle.

With a horseshoed beach,
a black sandy shore
affording safe harbour
for the frigate to moor.

Anchored in bay
at last seaman's penance,

sea's salty tang slips
into terra's sweet fragrance.

The scent of the land,
lush flora teases,
fruit trees and orchids
on tropical breezes.

A welcoming throng
arrives shouting rants.
Muscular warriors
bellow their chants.

A cold, dreadful fear
displaces amour,
as long oaken oars
row a skiff to the shore

Eight strong men
with a throne on their shoulders,
sit it down with the king
revered by beholders.
Salutations exchanged,
a more amiable throng,
drums' cadence elicits
a welcoming song.

While out-rigger canoes
traverse surf's huge waves

to welcome our craft
with hospitable raves.

Young damsels toss garlands,
wear only a smile
and short grass skirts,
the dress of the isle.

Shore leave arranged
for evening *luau*.
Shipmates well-groomed
debark the ship now.

Through palm trees with coconut,
past tropical flowers
whose sweet scent enchants,
then overpowers.

Perfumed fragrance
quickly replaced
by culinary spices,
a buffet is showcased.

Wild boar roasting
on a slow-turning spit.
Red tuna in lime juice
simmer in a pit.

Breadfruit and sweet yams,
king and guests dine

with taro root pudding,
his banquet's divine.
Pulsating drums
drive maidens to dance.
Throbbing hips stir
primordial trance.

Bronze coloured *danseur*,
all save but one.
Much fairer toned hue
whose beauty can stun.

She captured my soul.
Brown eyes so dreamy,
cropped auburn hair,
smooth skin so creamy.

Partners are chosen
by placing a nose
on the cheek of the man
they want for their beaus.

Floret in hair,
lavender blue.
Slowly approaching,
she comes into view.

Sparkling smile
slaying me dead.

My heart lays prone.
Resistance has fled.

Shot with desire,
her scent will compel.
Surrender complete,
It's *La Vie Est Belle*?

Ice cool paradise
just kisses away.
She presses her nose,
then fades away
My cheek is poked.
Harder again!
Fasten your seat belts,
Papeete in ten.

Eyes half-open.
Where am I? Not sure.
It's the girl from my dream.
Ah! —paramour.

The Cliché

I wrote this poem for a good friend that hates clichés.

Forlorn phrase
Poetic outcast
Poets warned
To avoid it like the plague.

If used
The poets work
Arrives
Dead as a doornail.

Avoid the scorned maxim
Shun the disdained adage
The bard's labour flourishes
All's well that ends well.

Perhaps not!
Maybe the idiom

is not so worn.
Take the tiger by the tail!

Use the well-used
If it fits
Take advantage of
Low hanging fruit.

Oh, tired expression
You are not so boring
That you should box in
Think outside the box!

Breath life into
The writer's work
Accentuate humour
Laughter is the best medicine

But at the end of the day
Every cloud has a silver lining
Time will tell
If we all live happily ever after.

The Ember is Out

A love affair like a Roman candle ends as abruptly as it began.

Pickles to roses
moving through thorns.
Sweet fragrance drifting
across notes from horns.

Cherries exploding
vivid flashes of light
illumine this cave
once dim, now bright.

Soaring soul sings
a rapturous song,
deeply evocative,
resonantly long.

Timeless passion
it fails but not

arduous will
'till friction's too hot.

The fragrance? It fades.
Together, yet nixed.
Lapsing bouquet,
passions are mixed.

Rhapsody meets
the Reaper upon
bleak killing fields
where amity shone.

Icy dour winds
blow round about
silent soma reeking.
The ember is out.

The Letter B

The Letter B is a nonsensical alliteration poem using the letter B.

Birding bird-dogs
Best block backlogs
Being bereft but battling bulldogs
Bring buzzards belonging by bogs
Brimming barrage budding bullfrogs.

Behest banning bodily broth begat
Busy blue bobcat
Bobbing black-bellied bat
Barring breathing brat
Butting baffling brickbat.

The Unjust Society

A "Just Society" was called for by the father, extolled by the son, yet unfulfilled.

We appeal to all, reconcile—
TRCC[3]
A plea from first people willing
to governments averse.
Words that echo down empty halls
only to land upon stopped up ears.

We call upon these governments,
to adopt and effect
the declaration
UNDRIP[4]
Issued by that august league.
Rejected by four
disobedient sons,
colonial nations,

---

3   TRCC, Truth and Reconciliation Commission Canada
4   UNDRIP, United Nations Declaration on the Rights of Indigenous Peoples

peoples unable
to be just.
O Canada, codify.
Initiate reconciliation.

We will; we will
exclaimed the lesser.
A campaign pledge
soon to be broken.
A stump vow
fulfilling that promise
the elder espoused
so long ago.
A Just Society— NOT!

WITS Limericks

WITS is a writers' group that asks its members to write limericks for its annual Christmas dinner. These are my contribution. 2018

There once was a woman named Bird
Who did not like what she heard
The City Council, it seems
Was destroying her dreams
Of low taxes with no antics absurd.

The poor mayor was under a siege
His council said he was their liege
Now Bird had a thought
Put in for a spot
Now council the plan to besiege.

The election was run right on time
Her name on the ballot, not mine
She ran, and she won

Now the work has begun
A new council and new paradigm.

2019

There once was a jackass named Trump
Who'd do anything he that he thunk
With the help of the Russians
But not of the Prussians
He stole an election - it stunk.

Ripping kids from the arms of their mothers
He put them in cages with others
Poor Muslims he banned
He decreed out of hand
Shithole countries would not have their druthers.

But a phone call would be his undoing
The Dems would now be pursuing
Impeach him they cried
And then he'll be tried
The thought of it left him just stewing.

About the Author

David D Plain is a historian/author. One of his books won a Golden Scribe award in 2008 and was a finalist for an Eric Hoffer Award in 2014. He has published four non-fiction history books and one historical fiction. David also published a poetry book, a memoir and co-authored the screenplay for a one-hour TV drama series based on his historical fiction.

Love Poems and Other Things is his second poetry book. It contains various forms of poetry, from free verse to sonnets. The love poems are intermingled with an eclectic theme from spirituality to nature. This existential collection is informed by events in David's life, making for a work that hits home.

Printed in the United States
by Baker & Taylor Publisher Services